A DATE
WITH YOUR
SOULMATE

An Emotional Instinct

A DATE WITH THE SOULMATE

An Emotional Instinct

SURESH K AGARWAL

PARTRIDGE
A Penguin Random House Company

To order additional copies of this book, contact
Partridge India
000 800 10062 62
www.partridgepublishing.com/india
orders.india@partridgepublishing.com

CONTENTS

Moral Tales

ABOUT THE AUTHOR

The author is a God-fearing man with sensitive and emotional nature. Though he is not a writer, he has dared to attempt—with the support of Partridge India in editing, publishing, and giving a helping hand—to climb the highest platform of Penguin Random House Company, London.

The author has given his best out of his life's experiences, which he has gone through, from good and bad, ups and downs, breakthrough and breakdown finances, deteriorated relationships, passion and compassions, success and failures, comforts and sufferings, innocence and overconfidence, and ultimately practically faced and learned the subjects in reality and morals and philosophies of life, ethics, and principles of business. These are the contents of the book.

This is for all the generations to correct themselves and not to suffer and commit the same mistakes and prosper and lead a life with dignity and die with dignity.

The people who bank on only luck will also not benefit and will waste their precious time waiting for windfalls. The efforts and luck runs parallel like the rail track equally. The author is also a firm believer of karma theory: do the best and live the rest and keep on doing without any expectations of the results of your doings. Play the character of the show to your best; you will be awarded, you will be rewarded, and you will be applauded. Under the influence of false ego, one thinks himself to be the doer of activities, while in reality all activities are carried out by nature as a natural process.

The author has seen the riches and spent lavishly on comforts, such as clothes and luxury cars, and was the frequent flyer and privilege cardholder of all the airlines. At the same time, he never felt to move on with a two-wheeler and with no credit cards. No bank balances, no protocols—an absolutely mediocre life.

The author passed through a severe depression stage when his industries were shut down, auctioned by bankers, and he was imprisoned by the authorities for forty-five days for charges of tax evasion and for amassing wealth in a short term. Therefore, ability without dependability, responsibility, and flexibility is a liability. People without conviction do not take a stand. They go along to get along because they lack confidence and courage. Some people consider themselves a shade better because they do not support the wrong; however, they lack the conviction to oppose. But by not opposing something you know is wrong, you are actually supporting it. And here I end by saying,

> "If you can, you will, and
> If you can't, you will never."

And finally, my inspirational lines which inpired me to write:

> "If you write something, it should be worth reading, and if you can't, then do something worth writing."

GOLDEN WORDS

If you fail to plan, you are planning to fail.

Planning without action is futile.
Action without planning is fatal.

Success is simple—Do what's right, the right way at the right time.

No sound in this world can be more louder than silence and if any one cannot understand your silence they can never understand your word.

You have a right to "Karma" (actions) but never to any fruits thereof. You should never be motivated by the results of your actions, nor should there be any attachment in not doing your prescribed activities. (duties).

There are no secrets to success. It is the result of preparation, hard work and learning from the failure.

Success does not lower its standard to accommodate us, we have to raise our standard to achieve it!

For every bird God provides food but not nest. You have to build it by yourself, let it take time, it will not be available ready made to you.

When you do anything new, at first people laugh at you, then they challenge you, then they watch you succeed and then they wish they were you.

Our task now is not to fix the blame for the past, but fix the course for the future.

Destiny is not a matter of chance, it is a matter of choice, it is not a thing to be waited for, it is a thing to be achieved.

When your Signature becomes autograph it means—you are successful.

EFFORTS

He worked by the day.
And toiled by the night.
He gave up play,
And some delight.
Dry books he read,
New things to learn.
And forged ahead,
Success to earn.
He plodded on with,
faith and pluck.
And when he won,
men called it luck.

I am not the one who bank upon luck, and not afraid of those who rely on it. I see luck as an opportunity to work harder.

He slept beneath the moon,
He basked beneath the sun,
He lived a life of going to do,
and died with nothing done."

"Achievers never expose themselves,
but their achievements expose them,
Do or die was an old saying,
Do before you die is the new one.

A paper flying in air is due to luck, but a kite flying in air is due to your efforts! So don't worry if luck doesn't support efforts will work.

LUCK

Journey of life starts with a full bag of luck and an empty bag of experience. The goal is to fill the bag of experience before the bag of luck gets empty!

— ⟋⟍ —

You cannot change your future, but you can change your habits. And surely your habits will change your future.

— ⟋⟍ —

Takdir he khel se Nirash nahi hote,
Zindagi mein kabhi udas nahi hote,
Haatho ki lakiro par yakin mat karna,
Takdir to unki bhi hoti hai jinke haath nahi hote.

— ⟋⟍ —

Everything about the future is uncertain,
But one thing is sure, God has already arranged all our tomorrows, we just have to trust him today.

—◆—

Destiny is simply the strength of your desires.
If you cry at trouble, it grows double.
If you laugh at trouble, it disappears like a bubble.
This is how you can be the creator of your own Destiny!

—◆—

If everything is going according to your wish then you are lucky, if not, then you are too lucky because it is going according to God's wish.

—◆—

"If you write something it should be worth reading, or if you can't do something worth writing".

—◆—

Nobody Is Destiny's Child

Information
(feedback, hearing, knowing, learning,
understanding, seeing)
↓
Thoughts
(positive, negative, optimist, pessimist,
practical, unpractical)
↓
Feelings
(hurt, pain, sorrow, happy, energetic,
enthusiastic, overwhelmed)
↓
Actions
(physical work, verbal, writing,
doing, designing, operating)
↓
Habit

(repetitive act, daily routine, performing
on a daily basis, etc.)
↓
Character
(labelling, judging, analyzing, blaming,
ethics, morale, principles)
↓
Destination
(decide to do something, desire to
reach fulfilment/succeed)
↓
Destiny
↓

The present is the result of your past, and also the present will be the result of your future. So don't waste your present; your present is nothing but a happening, which is happening right now. So be in the complete present which is full in itself. Do not try to be attached with your past nor future; it will also spoil your present. Past brings tears, future brings fears, whereas the present is the only one who brings cheers! So enjoy the present which will become the past as you enter it, and don't worry about the future as we don't even know about it, then why fear it? Be always wholly in the present, which is in your hands. The past is like a shot arrow from a bow. The future is the stocks of arrows on your back. The present is the arrow ready on the bow. Now aim it properly on your target, and you will reach the goal. If you use your arrow to kill or hurt someone, it will get you the same result, and if you choose to save or relieve someone, it will get you the same result. Life is like a valley; your actions will echo the same. If you hurt somebody, somebody will hurt you, and if you save somebody, somebody will save you at the time of pain and sorrows of life. This is called the karma theory: that somebody is nobody but you yourself. So the option given to us is the arrow on the bow; use it with utmost care, use it with grace, use it with tactfulness, use it with a kind heart, but not to exhibit your power or skills by hurting the innocent. Do not be influenced by the mind, but always listen to your heart. The mind is a plotter, whereas the heart is innocent, full of love and sacrifice. If you choose to relieve, you will be relieved from all the pains and sorrows. Shri Krishna says, "Vruthi pravakthi vruthaha" which means "Thoughts are changed you are relieved from pain". So your thoughts are the seeds to your actions; use them judiciously, and one day you will become somebody from nobody, and once you become somebody, your signature will become an autograph—it means you are successful in achieving your goal!

The Lust for Comfort
Murders the Passion
of the Soul

One of my favourite Robin Sharma, who noted, "The reasonable man adapts himself to the world; the unreasonable one persists in trying to adapt the world to himself. Therefore, all progress depends on the unreasonable man." Please think about that idea for a moment. I suggest it's a big one.

Sure, be practical and operate intelligently as you move through your world. I agree, it's important to use common sense. True, foolish risks can lead to difficult consequences. But having said that, don't be so scared of failure and disappointment that you fail to dream. Don't always be so reasonable and practical and sensible that you refuse to seize glorious opportunities when they show up. Push the envelope as to what's possible for you. Remember critics have always laughed at the visions of bold thinkers and remarkable visionaries. Ignore them. And know that every outstanding piece of human progress was achieved through the heroic efforts of someone who told them their ideas were impossible to realise. The world needs more dreamers. Unreasonable souls who fight the urge to be ordinary, who resist the seduction of complacency and doing things the way they have always been done. You can be one of them. Beginning today.

The lust for comfort murders the passion of the soul. The dreamers who don't sleep and who work hard without worrying about the results are the real heroes, and I salute the heroic efforts of unreasonable man.

Beware: Bitterness Kills

People who are affected identify its taste, which is neither sweet nor salty but bitter—that is why depressions are intrinsically associated to the word "bitterness".

All beings have bitterness in their organism—to a greater or lesser degree—in the same way that almost all of us have the tubercle bacillus (TB). However, these two diseases only attack when the patient is debilitated; in the case of bitterness, the terrain for the disease to arise appears when we are afraid of the so-called reality.

Certain people, in their anxiety to build a world where no outside threat could penetrate, increase exaggeratedly their defences against the outside—strangers, new places, different experiences—and leave the inside unprotected. It is then that bitterness begins to cause irreversible harm. People attacked by this evil begin lose their desire for everything and, in a few years, are unable to go outside their world because they have used up enormous energy reserves building high walls for the reality to be what they wanted it to be. When avoiding outside attack, they also limit internal growth. They continue going to work, watching television, complaining about the traffic, and having children, but all that happens automatically, without really understanding why they are behaving like that. After all, everything is under control. The great problems of bitterness are passions, love, hate, enthusiasm, and curiosity, which don't appear any more. The chronically bitter person only notices his disease once a week—on Sunday afternoons. Then, as he has no work or routine to relieve the symptoms, he realises that something is very wrong.

However, the cause for the bitterness would not be the same for every patient, and therefore, the treatment cannot be the same.

But the medication is not only a good sound sleep; the major therapies are love, affection, attachment, acceptance, counselling, and encouragement.

The number of failures, humiliation, anxiety, and tragic moments in life are the major reasons for the cause of this bitterness, so please be very fragile with the person or he may get hurt though your intention would not be to hurt him. These persons adapt to a very narrow side of life and simply take anything and everything to heart—their thoughts become very presumptive and their perceptions remain abusive.

Not last but least, the critics of the heroes are awarded as bitter.

> "Forgive the other person but don't forget their name".

CELESTIAL BLISS

Celestial bliss is also known as Amruth Kalash—the pot of treasures for which Devas and Asuras were fighting to grab whatever comes out of it one by one. So have a look at who got what and see what you got the most.

Devas	Asuras
Happiness	Anger
Joyful	Frustration
Satisfaction	Irritation
Love	Fear
Gratitude	Anxiety
Innocence	Greed
Encouragement	Lust
Forgiveness	Guilt
Compassion	Regret
Empathy	Resentment
Creativity	Suffering
Inspiration	Destruction

Motivation

Apathy

Courage

Knowledge

Devotion

Willpower

Enthusiasm

Excitement

Passion

Confidence

Clarity

Sympathy

Apologise

Cooperation

Coordination

Understanding

Patience

Serenity

Compatibility

Sacrifice

Energy

Sharing

Caring

Humble

Meditate

Superiority

Comparison

Jealous

Self-doubt

Laziness

Ego

Dominate

Lovelessness

Power greed

Blaming

Deserted

Hurt

Rejected

Betrayal

Ignorance

Insult

Humiliation

Pain

Lethargic

Lack of confidence

Insecurity

Reluctant

Rigid

Overconfidence

Proud

This chapter is for everyone to score more and correct themselves and to be known as Devas or Asuras.

Passion and Compassion

We know what passion is; hence, it is not very difficult to understand what compassion may be. Passion means a state of biological fever—it is hot. You are almost possessed by biological, unconscious energies. You are no longer your own master; you are just a slave.

Compassion means you are no more a slave; you are a master. Now you function consciously.

> Passion is lust; compassion is love.
> Passion is desire; compassion is desirelessness.
> Passion is greed; compassion is sharing.
> Passion wants to use others as means;
> compassion respects others as an end to himself.

Passion keeps you tethered to earth, to mud, and you never become a lotus. Compassion makes you a lotus. You start rising above the muddy world of desires, greed, and anger. Compassion is transformation of your energies.

When all these energies are not wasted, you become full. A great delight arises in you. "Compassion is the ultimate transformation of passion. You are in passion, but you go on thinking that you are right as you are. You go on defending yourself. And anything that disturbs your comfortable, mechanical life. You go against, you love to be alone, you love to—meditate."

"Be passionate but one day finally you will love to be compassionate".

LEARN TO FAIL

We think failure is bad. It is not. It's good. No, it's great. There can be no success without failure. It's just part of the process.

The companies and people who have reached the heights of success are the same ones that have failed the most often. You need to fail to win. And the faster you fail, the more quickly you'll learn precisely what you need to do to win. So fail fast. Outfail the competition. Outfail the person you once were.

> "Only those who dare to fail greatly can ever achieve greatly".

A kid asked Swami Vivekananda, "Sab kuch kohne se Jyada bura kya hai?"

Swamiji replied, "Woh umeed khona, jiske Bharose par hum sab kuch vapas pa saktehai".

But after saying so, I feel it is necessary to tell about failure as nothing but the repetition of the same act again and again and not learning from the past and not correcting the present which leads to the next failure. If you start learning from the failure, it becomes the steps to your success. And every failure in life is like a step ahead to your success. So fail faster, learn faster, and be successful!

Happy success!

SUFFERING

One of the most deeply hidden reasons for suffering is that you may be enjoying it. For example, falling ill can become a source of pleasure if it gets you the attention and care you have been craving for. In the same way as a seed has to rupture before a plant can grow and blossom, intense suffering can rupture your ego and leave you open and vulnerable to transformation. Suffering has tremendous potential to integrate and transform us. Suffering is not a state of mind. It is not an event in your life. It is your response to an event. Never curse the pain or the person inflicting the pain on you. Instead, take the opportunity to use it as a blessing, watch objectively, and cut the root of the pain. Pain can be a great teacher if you allow it to be. If you properly research the cause and effect of pain within you, it can turn out to be the biggest turning point in your life.

Every suffering is like a seed and caterpillar; like a seed, suffering can propel you to become a plant and blossom, and like a caterpillar, suffering can propel you to rupture and fly like a colourful butterfly!

Be blissful!

INTENSITY

Intensity is not an emotion. When you are intense, one part of it may be emotional. Intensity should become a quality in you. If you are talking, let intensity be there. In your relationships, in your decisions, in your desires, even in your fears, be intense without escaping from this moment. Intensity does not depend on the nature of work or action. It can be as complex as running a billion-dollar company or as simple as cleaning the floor. It is not *what* but the *how* that is important. Intensity means radiating the energy that does not create any conflict inside and outside. Intensity is intensely being inside you. Intensity flows smoothly and yet strongly.

INTENT

A desire, an idea, an intention with emotional desire is called intent: to do something from the bottom of the heart. If you are passionate about something, then the whole universe will help you to make it happen. If your efforts are in one direction and the desire is in the opposite direction of your stand, then it will not work out, and your intent will remain unfulfilled. So pay attention to the goal and focus with consistent efforts; sacrifice your emotional and physical quest, give up some pleasures, and take some short-term pains to materialise your intent. With lots of effort inputs without diverting focus, you will be a receiver at the end of it. And finally, you turn the tables around.

Resentment

The person concerned, perceiving injustice, wrongs, or ingratitude nurtures a vague hope that his antagonism (opposition) and intimidation (forcefully) would bring change of heart on the other person or situation. But this imagined cure is worse than the disease. This unabated resentment is a deadly poison to the spirit, making happiness impossible, and uses up tremendous energy, which could go into accomplishment. Such resentments are manifest signs of self-image of not just a pitiful person, a victim, who was meant to be happy but also one who needs unfavourable and hostile situations around him as alibis and excuses to justify this self-image chosen for himself.

Resentment arises due to various reasons:

— missing of opportunities,
— difficult times faced earlier,

— facilities denied or disappointments,
— annoyance over unfairness all around.

A very common manifestation of such resentments or grudges, however, is anger over ingratitude or lack of appreciations. These damaging feelings, even when justified, have to be erased through comprehension of certain truths. Forget them and forgive them, you will be blessed twice. Don't feel restless, be blissful, and be happy!

> "Make a mind which never minds,
> Make a heart which never hurts,
> Make a touch which never pains,
> and make a relation which never ends."

HURT

Hurt starts with the habits which irritates—the way you eat, the way you talk, the way you look, the way you respond. Irritation becomes the cause of hurt. Initially, the irritation which you hold on to your feelings and start hating the person and by saying you hurt me. Anything starts with irritation, and if you don't resolve the same, you start judging people by labelling them—like childish, immature, rude, clever, non-committal, dominative, etc.— and it grows into anger and thereby start arguments, conflicts, differences, then no conversations, then the hurt is so deep you stop talking to each other.

PAIN

When you are hurt, you develop pain and sufferings and strain yourself; you start thinking, your emotional pattern gets disturbed, and you stop focusing on work, and this results in no creativity, no energy, no enthusiasm in business resulting in failures. And while all this is going on, the children are the most affected victims of the hurt and pains which we are passing on to them, and they start adopting the same pattern without love and affection. They grow up serious in nature and with lack of confidence and happiness. "Every painful story has a successful ending. Accept the pain & get ready for success".

"Every successful person has a painful story,
then you need not worry you are also one."

Principles of Business

A—attention, administration, advertisements, association, ambience, audit

B—branding, broad-minded, buying capacity, banking, balance sheet

C—costing, coordination, customer care, cooperation, correspondence, confidence, courageous, considerable, counselling, clarity, clear, clean

D—discounts, delivery, duty, development, duties, dealers, distributors

E—ethics, enthusiasm, exhibitions, extra time, extra cautious, exemptions

F—fair, fearless, fees, fire equipped, fuel, filtration, filing, formula

G—genuine, guarantee, guidance, government guidelines, graphs

H—honesty, human resources, hardship, high profile, humble

I—integrity, incentives, internship, international, ideology

J—joint venture, joint meeting, judicious, judgemental

K—kind, know-how, knowledge

L—labour-oriented, lasting relations, long-lasting, leverage, loans, licences

M—morals, motivation, meetings, marketing, maintenance

N—negotiations, nice

O—operations, occasional, overflow, overhead, office

P—principles, payments, purchases, prompt, publicity, presentations, packing, profits, pricing, productions

Q—quality, quantity, quotations, quarrelessness

R—research, right, renewals, recycling, registrations, records, resources

S—secrecy, sales, schemes, security, skills, subsidy, salaries, statistics, size, shape, strength, style, shine, sincerity, statements

T—timely commitments, target, trust, taxes, technology, trade fairs, training

U—ultimate, uniform, uniqueness, user-friendly, understanding

V—validity, velocity, volume, vehicles, visiting cards, visiting time

W—workmanship, work-oriented, workaholic, water resource, wastage

X—Xerox, x-linked dominant inheritance, x-linked recessive inheritance

Y—yearly, yield, yardstick

Z—zeal, zero, zodiac

These are not words; these are the qualities and responsibilities of a good administrator who has to take care of so many subjects while administrating. Therefore, he is the gem of the country who generates revenues, generates employment, gives taxes and duties, pays interest to the bankers, enriches the flourishing of the distributors and dealers, takes care of the customers' taste and choice, maintains stocks, maintains books of records, and complies with the government policies of the state and India. I therefore salute the administrator who takes so much of the pains and gives his best efforts, keeping his family aside and leaving the pleasures of the world, to serve you from early morning till midnight. Truly aspiring!

RELATIONSHIP

Needless to say, parents contribute to form a relation—father, mother, in-laws—but this is only one-sixth part of the share. To know more how the total share pattern of the entire relationship circle looks like:

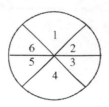

1. Parents—father, mother, in-laws
2. Spouse—wife
3. Relatives, friends, colleagues
4. Children
5. Self
6. Authority—senior in post

CAUSES OF DETERIORATED RELATIONSHIP

Expectations, lack of respect, conflicts, lack of connections, lack of communication, hurt, rejection, dejection, hatred, confrontations, frustrations, depression, and irritation in the relations are the major causes of deteriorated relationships. "Trust is the base of every relation. A small mistake can change its entire meaning—missing letter 'T' in Trust can 'Rust' the relations."

POWER OF BONDING
RELATIONSHIP

If this area is strong enough, no crisis, no recession, no economic failures, nothing can affect you. Unless and until you have a strong bond in the family, you will never come up in life because the family is the only one that will encourage you, nurture you, hold your hands to make your project a success, and rest will try to destruct and create obstacles in the path. So please give lots of time to the relationship. By doing so, you are not wasting time but you are ploughing and cultivating that which will grow and give you the fruits of affection and attachment, a strong hand to hold whenever you need it. This will lighten your stress. Frequently talking to them will encourage you to perform well in your daily tasks and improve your performance day by day. They will correct you where you are misguided or misled by your opponents. Relationships are nature's gifts—it is not by your choice but it is always the choice of God, so try to respect the gift of God. Love them from the bottom of the heart!

> Quote: The Real measure of relation is not when two people like each other, it's when one ignores and the other continues loving with a silence till the end.

BREAKTHROUGH AND BREAKDOWN FINANCES

Every person must be involved and indulge in creating wealth or generating it as an intensely religious act. But at the same time, making money is sin, which is only possible in gambling, horse racing, forward trading, or other bad habits of making money (Mcx, cricket, etc.).

Wrong investments in wrong ventures, real estates, and wrong people lead you to debts and will create breakdown finances. Rolling or rotating the money wisely is called a breakthrough finances situation. Right emotions will bring you right contacts; wrong emotions will bring you wrong contacts and wrong habits of making money and results in a breakdown of emotions. And breakdown of emotions start conflicting inside. It is nothing but the fear inside, blaming others, and lack of confidence. In every second, 50,000 cells die and are produced as we think they develop in the same line and then they multiply, creating a depression-like situation. Have a right emotion without conflict or guilt; you will be high in the air, and you will be a different person, a different individual to whom people like admiring, adoring, and liked by one and all.

MIND IS A SINNER

We are the creators of our thoughts, our feelings, and our emotions. These are the three elements which disturb you and hurt you. If you are taking them deep into the heart, then assume that you are flown away by the creations of the mind. We must protect them by shielding ourselves by saying that "It is not me who can be disturbed by the thoughts or feelings. It is not me who can be flown away by the emotions because I am a soul, and all these are the creations of the mind. The mind is a sinner, not me." The soul is sacred and serene, whereas thoughts, feelings, and emotions are dreadful diseases generated by the mind. So be careful; don't allow yourself to nurture them in you. Eradicate them by meditating, shielding by chanting "OM SHANTI OM". Then you are fully protected from inner as well as outer criticism or guilt. Look as if you are an audience to the drama and watch every person as a character. Don't try to change them, nor try to judge them.

Be a patient audience, and enjoy the play by feeding them in your consciousness.

> "To handle yourself use your mind, and to handle others, use your heart."

DETERMINATION

We find people who literally wander through life. They simply accept whatever fate brings them. A few may succeed by accident, but the most suffer through a lifetime of frustration and unhappiness. This is not for them, but it is for those who have determination to succeed and willingness to devote the time and effort necessary to achieve success.

To start an action plan for the rest of your life, focus on the purpose and generate new ideas about yourself and the future. Your attitude also contributes to success in achieving your goal. When our attitude is right, we realise that opportunity is always under our feet. We don't have to go anywhere; all we need to do is recognise it. Now use your character, integrity, good values, and positive attitude and work or adapt in practical theories of doing things and have the right feelings, right relationships, and put in your efforts. A focused determination and intense,

39

result-oriented, purpose-driven, massive action plan, which is time bounded with lots of grace, determines your determination. And with this determination you are bound to succeed!

CERTAINTY AND UNCERTAINTY

Certainty is nothing but a type of feeling. If you are certain, it means you are comfortable, safe, and secured, but the vice versa feeling of certainty is insecurity, fearfulness, and uncomfortableness (uncertainty). Life does not come with anything certain. Change is the law of life, but challenge is an aim of life. So you have to challenge the changes but don't change the challenges. Changes that happen do not entail time is second changes happen. Life is like a ball; the deeper you fall, the higher you bounce back.

Nothing in this world is going to be as per your wish; it requires proper planning and meticulous efforts to keep everything in place (certainty). But certainly certainty is the key to happiness, but you have to crave for it by building your thoughts like every brick counts when we build a house. To build a good character, every thought counts, so be positive and feed the mind daily with positive thoughts.

The most important factor to keep certainty is do not make any small or big decisions on the basis of your mood. A mood is a dangerous state of mind because it can crush the reason under the weight of feelings. Always whatever decision you take in life must be reasonable, less risky, less expectations, and more practical. It should be, otherwise extra hopes will get you more disappointments and uncertainty.

A single wrong decision could make your life miserable. Life's critical decisions are to be evaluated before you decide. The process of evaluation should include the following things: (1) what I am doing, (2) what the result might be, and (3) will I be successful. Those who ignore the evaluation process are uncompleted to have failure, or you may be deceived.

If you are deceived once and if you fail once, it does not matter, but if it is happening again and again, then you are a fool, and you alone are held responsible for your mistakes, and therefore learn from failure and correct them for not repetition in life. If you start learning from failures, the failures become your steps to success. Those who stare at the past have their backs turned to the future, thereby making your every single decision, however small or big, more important or less important. Give a second thought to it and proceed. Uncertainty will disappear from your life, or say certainty will prevail in your life and go back to the first paragraph—certainty is nothing but a feeling of comfort, safety, and security, and insecurity, fearfulness, and uncomfortable feelings would disappear from your life forever.

"Be certain in life"!

CONFIDENCE

When you start up any project or any work, you should know what you are doing and you should do it with utmost interest and intensity, and if you are following this, then you are confident. But vice versa, if you are starting anything new without any knowledge about what you are going to do and if you are not putting your mind with any interest, then it will surely bring you lack of confidence. And if you are doing any venture without evaluation, only with presumption and assumption, and you are doing it with the purpose of showing off in society or the trade, then surely it is overconfidence. Confidence brings success, lack of confidence brings humiliation, and overconfidence brings failures.

Confidence comes by proper focus, 100 per cent effort, total survey of the project, and meticulous planning. An action plan and time frame will surely give you confidence to tackle the obstacles in your venture and strength to fight back your opponents to give everybody a shock on your

43

successful achievements. So be confident and make your dreams into reality and rise up to the challenges; face them boldly with instinct and righteous decisions without any conflicts in mind and clarity in your thoughts!

ABOUT MYTHS OF PLANETS AND VASTHU

The universe is with several solar systems. And one solar system with so many planets, movements of planets' rotation, revolution, and creates rays, which affect our mind and thereby our thoughts and thoughts into action, and the result is the reaction of our actions. Alpha and beta rays—or say positive or negative, or say malefic or benefic rays—accordingly the body system functions and feels as per the reflections of the rays. Generally, the energy is produced by the movements of the planet from one place to another. It creates changes. Cosmic energies are good and bad, favourable and unfavourable, auspicious and adverse influences on the natives; therefore, astrology is the science of the movement of planets and calculations which evaluates the good and bad period coming ahead as per the movement calculations.

Vasthu is the science of air, water, earth, and fire, elements: the flow and directions of the air and water, the elevation and slopes of earth, the frequency of the fire and waves as per universe system. To flow with the universe, the measure adapted would be beneficial and does not create any obstacles and not disturb the waves' frequencies, thus helping to get maximized and be benefited by it scientifically is called Vasthu Shastra which was followed by Vishwakarma, the Architect and Engineer of the Hindu Gods.Hence, the concept of Vasthu has become the tradition in India.

LIVE WITH PRIDE, NOT WITH PROUD

Living with pride is great, the conscious mind knows. Pride in other words signifies dignity, humility, and honour. If you are doing whatever is touched by your heart, that is pride. Like if you are nursing your ailing mother, caring for your aged father, loving your wife and children, respecting your religious traditions, talking with humbleness to your colleagues, and honouring your mentors or teachers, it is pride.

Living proud is exhibiting your power, position, wealth, knowledge, and appearances. Being proud, in other words, is misusing the gift that God showed you. If you are not in a conscious mind, it means you are in a subconscious mind, which arises when you are overdrunk. Being proud is more or less dangerous and intoxicating; it could lead to fatalities. Excess of drink or excess of power, excess of misuse of knowledge to fool others is fooling yourself. So it is better to be smart rather than to be extra smart.

Anything in excess is dangerous; be in a conscious state of mind and live your life with pride instead of falling on roads after high intoxicants. Live a life with dignity and humility; you will be elevated to great heights!

No One Is
a Born Billionaire

According to the world's hundred richest people today, twenty-seven are heirs and seventy-three are self-made. Of the self-made, eighteen have no college degrees and thirty-six are children of poor parents, and some billionaires had neither a degree nor wealthy parents. In other words, super achievers are not born; they are self-made people. It is not external favour that makes one a superachiever but one's own struggle. Superachievement is not gotten through inheritance but is self-acquired success.

No one is born a billionaire, but everyone is a potential billionaire. It is the unfolding of one's own potential that makes one a billionaire or a superachiever. Nature does not discriminate between one person and another; nature's gifts come to everyone equally. It is the receiver himself who either utilizes them or not.

So-called deprived persons are in fact privileged persons. Their state of deprivation serves as inner motivation. When they see others are progressing, it creates a strong incentive in their minds. It is this incentive that makes a person super. It articulates a strong urge in the individual to make something of his life.

Any state of deprivation brings about a kind of brainstorming which enhances the inner spirit. They enter the world of competition; working to their full capacity, they develop the spirit of do or die. It is this spirit that leads them to success.

There is a saying that goes "Mr X was born with a silver spoon in his mouth". This kind of birth creates a kind of contentment in the concerned person, and this kind of contentment kills motivation. A silver or a golden spoon should develop a kind of discontent that ought to activate one's mind and trigger a fire within one to do hard work.

You can seldom find a family who started its history with a treasure of gold and diamonds. Forever the treasure of gold is a phenomenon of the future, not of the present. Every family initially started its history from rags and not from riches. The story of rags to riches is not the story of exceptional persons, but it is the story of every successful family or successful person.

One who is born in a state of affluence could become intellectually dwarfed, while one who is born in poor circumstances could emerge as an intelligent giant.

The law of nature is greater than everyone and everything else. They are eternal; they cannot be changed. The law of nature in this regard says that it is not else but effort, not facility but difficulty that makes achievers out of ordinary people. So the future is full of hope and opportunity—go and get it!

LEARN TO LEARN

Learning has no ages, no boundaries, nor any ending. Learning should be cultivated as a habit. One must be thirsty to know more. Have curiosity to learn whatever, whenever you can. In any field, learning should be a process if cultivated as a habit. It is knowledge, and knowledge is always wisdom.

If you are a self-employed or an employed, if you are a doctor or an engineer, if you are a politician or a bureaucrat—learning only always pays back. It costs nothing and pays back in abundance. If you are a wise planner and an economist, you will see the chart and graphs going up. It can be monetary gain or can result in growth and development of the society from the process of learning. Paying back to the society is always appreciated. Appreciation brings recognition, and recognition brings followers.

So first be a follower, and the rest will follow. To learn, you can surf, you can read, you can write, you can listen,

51

you can think, you can evaluate, and finally, you will be able to compile and make history.

And if you think learning is costly, it is better to be bankrupt rather than be a fool!

Inventions are the result of curiosity and knowing more and more. Without food and sleeping nights, with lots of daydreams, with passion to do something will ultimately result in something. "Do something, something will happen, and do nothing, nothing will happen." Always be with a great appetite to learn, be curious, be thoughtful, be creative, be fearless, be keen to know more and more. You will be worthy. And if you are worthy, then life is worth living. If you are content, you are conscious, and if you are conscious, you are close to the source and back to God.

Learning always begins from the day we come into the world with closed hands, and it continues every day till the final day of our journey back with opened hands. Closed hands are givers and opened hands are takers, and don't be a taker, be a giver. Giving is always bigger than taking. So think big, do big, learn big, give big, dream big, and from big to bigger and finally the biggest!

LACKING IS ALWAYS FAILURE

An entrepreneur succeeds not only because he had surplus money. Business does not only run on money criteria. The days have gone; putting capitals in the business is no more a criteria. The present trend is of new entrepreneurs without bank balance making millions, but if you lack money, no problem. Just don't lack in the following criteria:

1) Lack in foolproof survey of the project
2) Lack in meticulous planning about the project
3) Lack in determination and confidence in the project
4) Lack in team spirit and timeless effort for the project
5) Lack in present ability of your product
6) Lack in approach to your customer
7) Lack in accountability of the finances
8) Lack in administration and management
9) Lack in communication skills
10) Lack in quality and timely delivery
11) Lack in upgradeability of technology

12) Lack in exposure of the company
13) Lack in environment systems
14) Lack in customer satisfaction
15) Lack in research and development

If you don't lack, then you will be lucky, and people will recognize you as a leader. So don't worry. Go ahead; an idea can change your life!

IMAGE IS NOT BY DEFAULT

Any person or company or a brand is not created in a short while. Image is not by default; it is the blueprint of your impression created. A person's image is built by the appearance, the way you walk, the way you dress, the way you smell, the way you talk, the way you take decisions, the way you react to the situations, the way you participate in a social gathering, and the way you use your accessories. The impressions you have been doing in the past is your image in the present.

A company or a brand is like a child for 1,000 days or say three years. You have to nurture it with care, with a great patience, develop it, transform it, maintain it, continue it, market it, promote it, and if you complete the thousand days, then it means you have created a brand image. Now your product is familiar, and the product is saleable, the product is worth it, and the product is appreciable in the market. The appreciation is nothing but a brand image built in three years, which now you will have to maintain with the same quality which was appreciated by the customer. You have a choice to rename the product or change the packing of the product but not the content.

Happy branding!

DARE ARE THOSE WHO KNOW TO LOVE THEMSELVES

Loving any other is the easiest job, but loving self is the job of the bold. And those who dare are those who know to love themselves. They may not be loved by all, but they crave themselves. In criticism or appreciation, in breakthrough finances or breakdown finances, in situations under control or situations beyond control, they overshine one and all. They may be having lots of pains, but they will not reveal anything and start to share your problems and try to find out the solutions for your problems. They may be confused on their path of life, but they will be ready to guide you through your path if you feel you are confused. Loving self is selfishness. Loving self is taking the pain of others and not of self. Loving self is not taking but only giving. Loving self is broader in perspective and not narrow. Loving self is sacrifice and not comforts. Loving self is hunger and feeding others. Loving self is lotus and not cactus. Loving self is desert and not green lush. Loving self is devotion and not hatred. Loving self is peace and not impatience. Loving self is the most daring of all the bolder things in the world. So dare to love yourself.

PUPPET SHOW: THE WORLD

Yes, if you are thinking how the world can be puppet show, you are right. To know more precisely, read this:

First is that the puppet show consists of characters which are good and bad. Second is that the total show is managed on strings and proper timing to give its best effects. Think as the architect, creator, and player of the show. In the same way, the world also plays each and every one as a character in itself. All are managed by timing, from kids to executives, housewives to servants, engineers to doctors, astrologers to tarot readers, but the only thing common in both the show is the architect, creator, and player. He is at the back of the curtain. He is never seen. He is never appreciated. He is never exposed to the public. He is the key player of the entire show—he is invisible. He is known as Ram, Rahim, Nanak, and Jesus in places from north to south and east to west. For him there are no boundaries, no caste, no creed, no favour or disfavour. He, as per the character, gives the actions and as per actions he is being awarded—good or bad, king or beggar, weak or bold, ugly or beautiful, soft or hard. The creation is his choice. He chooses the character, he chooses the place, he chooses the time of entry, he chooses the action, he chooses the qualities, and he chooses the exit from the show. Isn't it, very strange but true, we are puppets in the hands of a master, and our strings are controlled by him. Therefore, we have no choice of anything to choose, so let us enjoy playing a character in the show. Who knows when our exit is from the show?

That's true, that's life!

INNOCENCE IS ADORABLE

Innocence is pure as water. Innocence is like a lotus. Innocence is like a peacock. Innocence is like an incense stick.

To magnify why innocence is pure as water, it is soft and flow swiftly as per the way and never stagnates at a place. It goes and mixes up with the lakes, rivers, and seas but never changes its attitude.

Innocence is like a lotus in the mud. No mud slings can stay on it because it is very fragile and stable. Therefore, it floats with the big base leaves slowly and steadily moves to the edges without any struggle or force.

Innocence is like a peacock, a colourful bird, very beautiful, and dances in the forest without any reasons. It is only the purest of all, like the god of all communities—Nanak, Krishna, Dargah. The male peacock weeps, and the female peacock takes the drop for conceiving and sacrifice is their reproduction cycle. Therefore, they are the purest of all and loved by all.

Innocence is like an incense stick; you light it at any place and it will give you the same smell, whether you place it in the puja room or the bedroom or at the bar or dargah. The smell never changes as per places, the duration does not change, nor does the appearance change. Changes are only external but not internal, so be innocent, be pure, be soft, be beautiful, be stiff, but always never forget your qualities.

Dad: A Smile for You

A great man who spares his life
Hides his feelings
Ignores his happiness
Accepts the pain
Forgets his comforts
Struggles in work

To make us live comfortably and happy in our life without any struggle, so wear a smile for your dad, which costs nothing, only a smile and makes him feel rejuvenated, and it will de-stress him. A small smile can do big wonders for him; he will be charged with more enthusiasm to work to make you feel more and more happy only at the cost of a smile and nothing else!

So

Smile <u>Please</u>

At no cost
Totally
100 per cent
Free

HOW HARD IT IS TO BE A FATHER

Don't take me wrong by the heading of the chapter. The man's mind is full of womanity and about sex. But it is not what you are thinking. It is about nurturing your son from day 1. From his birth, you start caring, loving, and buying each and every thing for his comfort and joy without his demand: from nappy to nipple, from dress to shoes, from bed to cradle to make him feel comfortable, beautiful, and joyous always. Nowadays growing a baby is a hard and costly job—from oils to soaps, creams to nutrients, from medicines to syrups. You cut down your budget of comforts and sacrifice. Thereafter you sacrifice your budget for his schooling, books, dress, fees, shoes, then after some years you cut down your budget more for his colleges, his jeans, T-shirts, pocket money, movies, and games. Then after he gets a good job, it is his time to pay back, and he starts with saying to his father, "Don't try to disturb me", "Don't try to dictate me", "Don't try to interfere in my life", then after he is married, he says, "Don't try to indulge with our family", and last but not least, he says, "Leave us alone". That's what the poor father gets the in payback after his lifelong sacrifices and cutting down his budget of his comforts: only abuse, abuse, abuse, and nothing else, and finally at his old age, he is left with no option and looks for a home for the aged and lives there the rest of his life.

MOTHER: THE ULTIMATE GOD

In reality no one in the world has seen God; we have been only told about him and what he was like. He did this and that and his name is so and so. But in reality, there is a god you have seen; you have felt her warmth, you have been fed by her with utmost care and hide, because she loved you more than herself. When you were young, she slept in your wet to make you sleep in the dry. She takes the pain for nine complete months and thereafter the whole life as long as she is alive. When you come in drenched from the rain, brother scolded, Father warned, sister shouted, but Mom, while drying your hair, said, "Stupid rain! Couldn't you stop till my child comes home?" When you grew up and got married and after you became a father, still you are a son to her, and when you come home from your business in the night, your wife asks about the sale, son asks about the profit, and Father asks about the payments, but Mother lastly asks, "Have you had your lunch?" This is called mother—the ultimate god.

"Azeez bhi woh hai naseeb bhi woh,
duniya ki bheed me kareeb bhi woh,
Iske Aashirwaad se chalti Zindagi,
Khuda bhi woh Aur Taqdeer bhi woh hai!"

"Koi rasta nahi duva ke siva,
Koi sunta nahi kuda ke siva,
Maine bhi zindagi ko karib se dekhahai,
Mushkil me koi saath nahi deta,
     MAABAAP KE SIVA!"

Love and respect your real god, and in turn, they will not ask for anything else from you.

"Is pyaar me bewafai ka jarokha nahi hota, har rishta itna Anokha nahi hota,
fana kardo zindagi maabaap ke kadmo me,
Quki yahi who pyar hai jisme Dhokha nahi hota."

"Mere Gunaho ko wo maaf kar deti hai,
Bahut gusse me hoti hai to bhi pyar deti hai,
Labo pe uske hameysha duva hoti hai,
Aisi sirf—"Maa hoti hai".

Zindagi mein do logo ka bahut khayal rakhna,

(1) Woh joh tumhari jeet ke liye bahut kuch hara ho (papa).

(2) Woh jisko tumne har dukh me pukaro ho
     (maa).

—☆—

The most beautiful thing in this world is to see
your parents smiling and the next best thing
is to know that you are the reason behind that
smile!

—☆—

Umid ko kabi khoya nahi karte,
Sahil agar dur ho to Roya Nahi Karte,
Rakhte hai jo dil me Tadap kuch pane ki,
Wo log to Raato ko bhi soya nahi karte.

—☆—

SISTERS: THE POWERHOUSE

You are the fortunate if God has blessed you with a sister, and with more sisters, you are more fortunate to have them. You are blessed with his abundance. If you have an elder sister, then she is known as your second mother, and if the sisters are younger, then they are the reason for your happiness. They are always there throughout the good and bad phases of life without any regrets. They always stand by you even if you are right or wrong and defend you. They are the powerhouse. They encourage and motivate you. They simply believe in you with blind eyes and never can hear anything adverse about you—however it is, whatever it is—they stand before you whoever is against you. Though they may be younger than you, at times they come when they feel you are not taking care of yourself; they become your grandma and feed you forcibly. They treat you like the father, and really it's very fortunate to have such good daughters (sisters). When in love you call them beta (daughter) more or less. Nothing more is precious in the world, nothing more is priceless in the world, nothing more is prestigious to have than sisters who are caring, loving, always there to share your emotions, always there to understand your feelings, always there to make you feel as if you are the best. Thank you, God, for such a beautiful and priceless gift to me. These are my assets in life. God, give me strength that I do not become a liability to them. Love you all from the bottom of the heart!

NEVER CHANGE THE THREE: BARBER, COUNSELLOR, DOCTOR

"**N**ever change the three" is also written in the old scripture of Hindus. The reasons for doing so are explained to you one by one.

Barber: The barber is the person who makes over your looks; he is the only person who knows what suits you the best. What should be the size of your sidelocks as per your face? What should be the cut of your hair and why? He is the person who decides and makes your appearance a pleasing personality, which is the first and foremost rule of a gentleman.

Counsellor: The counsellor is the person who knows about the mistake you have committed and proves that his client has not done anything wrong and proves you innocent. He knows the weakness of your opponent and keeps on hitting on it with so many rules and sections which finally proves him guilty and you as innocent.

Doctor: The doctor is the person who knows your body more than you. He knows what your body accepts and what does not. He knows what is your resistant capacity to which disease and which medicine suits you without any side effect to you while curing.

Therefore, always respect the three and never ever think of changing them as per your convenience or else it could get you humiliation, penalty, or fatalism in your life. Give your second thought for the three and you will know the importance of it, and deep thinking will surely prove that the point of explanations is true and correct.

Being Adventurous
means Fall on Face

Life is itself full of adventures, but the lust of more is dangerous—you might have seen the hoardings on the Highways saying "Speed thrills but kills" that true but we do not follow in practical life hence fall on face. Two young girls, Laukika and Samantha set off on an adventure. Both of them had completed their formal education and before venturing into their respective Samsaric enterprises, they thought of taking a break to contemplate life. Laukika was so overwhelmed with the idea of hedonistic idea of journeying and her own enthusiasm that she said to her friend. "I am going to jump into the river, Samantha and be carried along with its great energies. Meet you later". So saying, she took the plunge, without waiting for her friend to respond

Laukika enjoyed the initial adventure. At times the river frightened her, its strong current sweeping her along. But she dismissed her fears as she could now no longer see the shore. Laukika was euphoric and wanted more of the adventure. Forever engrossed in steadying herself from the speed of her journey. She managed mere fleeting glimpses of the beauty around her.

Now, the waves got bigger, the waters deeper, the river widened, the gusting became so forceful that she was thrown about, knocked about on the rocks all over, water and sand filled her nostrils and mouth, she was being bruised—by the gravel and creatures in the river "Help me to the shore. Someone". She cried, but no one heard her. Those who did hear her could not do much as they were not in a position to help her and finally one large wave thrown her on her face to the shore. Meanwhile, Samantha had set out on the foot,. "I choose to walk down the river bank instead. I might be able to enjoy the vistas better this way". She had thought to herself before embarking on her journey. Many years passed—The two friends met again. They hugged each other, happy to meet once again. Laukika admitted she did have her share of fun, but the journey had tired her out. Moreover she felt vacant inside. There was so much she wanted to do. She said but the sheer speed of her journey didn't permit her to take those liberties.

Samantha Spoke: "I too thought for long after you left me. Laukika I was tempted to follow you. The river looked enticing. But then, there was no hurry either I chose to walk down instead. I got to experience and enjoy the scenic offerings around the river. I marveled att the Sunrise and Sunset that were so different each day. The open blue sky was so re-assuring as were the stars at night. I played with the countless butterflies and birds that filled the forest. I stopped to smell the forest and baited with breath for the Kingfisher to dive into the water for a quick meal, and the Seagulls that flew over my head. I was tempted many times to plunge myself into the racing river, but would spend only a little time in the waters before drying myself on the warm rocks on the banks, read a book and resume my journey., The local people who collected firewood and fruits from the forest would invite me to their humble homes. I would play with their children and share with them simple tips on improving their health before bidding them goodbye. It has been an amazing journey.

The friends sat in silence, mulling over the choices they'd made and the experiences they'd been through.

You are Unique

Cosmic light is the basis of all beauty and diversity in the universe, as well as of all bio-diversity and life on earth. Each form of life is unique. Human beings the most evolved form of life, are most capable owing to especially evolved mind that controls the human phenomenon of being in Unison with cosmic powers of being an ally of the cosmos in its design of unfolding itself of creating new highs of creativity.

This uniqueness blossoming within every person is one the greatest wonders of universe light. This light writes the unique story of potential creativity in the mind of every one. What others have done so far, what other could not dare to do so far, you can do it. What specific thing you can do might be impossible for others to do. You can learn everything through your interaction with others, through attending classes in a University, through books and through media. Your common intellect helps you to learn everything you like to learn. But it is only the unique distribute nurturing itself within you which can help you invent, unfold and do something unique, something different from all others that you are a wonder in yourself. It is the unique attribute within you that can help you to reinvent yourself. It is the unique attribute shining within you can help you construct anew world and glitter within you and sparkle to new era of human creativity.

OPPORTUNITY

Doubtless, one who comprehends and applies the art of right timing, also seizing the opportunities, as they come, is also the one who divines that Supreme art of life and living.

What is actually opportunity—The face of the God which is concealed and it has wings on its feet, it is always unrecognized when it comes to you. "It is because men seldom recognize this God when it comes to them. He flies away soon and once gone, never comes back".

It is only possible by seizing the moment by doing the right thing at the right time and in a right manner. Whereby one is able to make the best of available resources. Even timely anger, when channeled well and rightly, could serve to galvanise a working force or the human resources, where gentle persuasion may fail. Of course anger with onself, attended with a steely determination to make up could be highly rewarded.At the same time tactful inaction or silence in certain situation could prove more powerful than reactions or responding. A great lesson for life is contained in every aspect of life. We should have the urge to learn, but not to wait for the opportunities while resourceful person make them. In deed, opportunity often knocks just once. Like an idea, this too has to be welcomed, entertained, nurtured and fashioned into a rewarding destiny.

The wish power and will power within, also rooted in effective and right—timing, could regardless of delayed efforts, be restored to for substantial fulfillment, instead resorting to passive repentance or regrets over a dead past.

Forget the past, work on present an so will be the outcome of your future. Don't wait for opportunity, create one, by doing right thing, in right direction, in right way and at the right time. Imply your innovative ideas and convert into reality. This is opportunity Grab it !.

The 20 Carefully Choosen Oneliners by Robin Sharma

(1)   Dream big. Start small. Act now.

(2)   Victims make excuses. Leaders deliver results.

(3)   Clarity breeds mastery.

(4)   Education is inoculation against disruption.

(5)   A problem is only a problem when viewed as a problem.

(6)   All change is hard at first, messy in the middle and gorgeous at the end.

(7)   If you are not scared a lot you are not doing very much.

(8)   Where victims see adversity. Extreme achievers see opportunity.,

(9)   The Project you are most resisting carries your greatest growth.

(10) Small daily improvements overtime lead to stunning results.

(11) Criticism is the price of ambition.

(12) Potential unexpressed turns to pain.

(13) Ordinary people love entertainment, extraordinary people adore education.

(14) Your daily behavior reveals your deepest beliefs.

(15) The only failure is not trying.

(16) Focus is more valuable than IQ.

(17) To double your income, triple your investments in self development.

(18) Your excuses are nothing more than the lies your fears sold you.

(19) An addiction to distraction is the end of your creative production.

(20) Life is short. Be of use.

15 Most Precious Quotes by Robin Sharma

(I)   "The Reasonable man adapts himself to the world,the unreasonable one Persists in trying to adapt the world to himself. Therefore all progress depends on the unreasonable man".

(II)   "People who have achieved great success are not necessarily more skillful on intelligent than others. What separates them is their burning desire and thirst for knowledge. The more one knows, the more one achieves".

(III)   "Your most challenging Relationship carries with it the seed of your greatest growth. The Relationship that tests, frustrates, irritates the most actually is one of your greatest blessing".

(IV)   "The Project that most scares you is the project you need to do first".

(V)   "Victims are frightened by the changes, leaders are inspired by the changes".

(VI)   Your two primarily Assets:
Your mental focus and your physical energy.

(VII) Excuses prevents us from taking action.

(VIII) With more awareness you can make better choices with better choices you will see better results.

(IX)   Complaining is worrying made verbal.,

(X)   The words you use in your sub-conscious mind. Rewire your beliefs.

(XI)   Remember that critics are dreamers one scared.

(XII) Fears unfaced becomes your limits.,

(XIII) Don't be the richest person in the graveyard, because health is wealth.

(XIV) Life is short. The greatest risk is risk-less living. And setting for a Average".

(XV)   Worries destroy your physical body and creativity of mind.

SOME IMPORTANT
DOS AND DON'TS

1. Avoid the three: pool of water, forest, and party. If unavoidable go for a while and come back.
2. Never make friends with people who are above or below you in status; such friendship will never give you any happiness.
3. A person should not be too honest. Straight trees are cut first, and honest people are screwed first.
4. Before you start some work, always ask yourself three questions:

    (a) Why am I doing it?
    (b) What the results might be?
    (c) Will I be successful?

Only when you think deeply and find satisfactory answers to these questions should you go ahead.

5. The biggest guru mantra is to never share your secrets with anybody. It will destroy you.

6. Once you start working on something, don't be afraid of failure and don't abandon it. People who work sincerely are the happiest.

7. Do not reveal what you have thought upon doing, but by wise counsel, keep it secret, being determined to carry it into execution.

8. In unfavourable situations, surrender to your enemy, but when time favours, break his head like a wet pot on the hard rock.

9. If your wife behaves like a mother in morning, by noon like a sister, and by night like a prostitute. Then you are lucky.

10. A book in the hand of a stupid is like a mirror in the hand of a blind.

11. If your son is a stupid, then amassing of wealth is waste, and if your son is intelligent, then also amassing the wealth is more waste.

12. If you are trying to please everybody, it means you are fooling yourself.

13. You will never reach your destination if you stop and throw stones at every barking dog. Better keep biscuits and move on.

14. Everyone is good to you till you expect nothing from them, and you are too good to them only till you fulfil their expectations.

15. A servant is tested at the time of work, relatives at the time of suffering, friends in calamities, and women during the loss of wealth.

16. Separation from one's wife, lack of respect from friends and relatives, a balance of loan, service to an evil king,

poverty, and a gathering of fools—all these burn the body without fire.

17. Sita was kidnapped because of too much beauty, Ravana was killed because of excess pride, King Bali was bound in ropes because of excess charity; therefore, always shun excess in anything.

18. No official is above greed. One without desire is not fond of beauty. An intelligent person cannot be a sweet talker, and a straightforward cannot be a crook.

19. A wise man should never reveal the following: a loss of wealth, a worry bothering his mind, faults of his household, having been made a fool by someone, and being humiliated.

20. One should be satisfied with the following three: one's own wife, food, and money.
One should be never satisfied with the following three: one's study, penance, and charity.

21. Whatever is given to an undeserving person, ignoring the deserving one, would be like giving something to an ass ignoring a cow.

22. The greatest fear in the world is of the opinions of others, and the moment you are unafraid of the crowd, you are no longer a sheep, you become a lion—a great roar arises in your heart, a roar of freedom!

23. No one is above the law and at the same time no one is below it.

1. Moral: We listen to what we want to hear and not what is said.

A medical doctor was giving a lecture on how the liquor is injurious to health, and to prove this, he had two glasses— one with distilled water and the other with alcohol in it. He put an earthworm into the distilled water; it swam beautifully and came up to the top. He put another earthworm into the alcohol, and it disintegrated in front of everyone's eyes. He wanted to prove that this was what alcohol did to the insides of our body. He asked the group what the moral of the story was, and a person from behind said, "If you drink alcohol, you won't have worms in your stomach", and the spectators laughed, and he concluded the speech. The person saying that was a selective listener. We hear what we want to hear and not what is being said, so please listen to what is not said and don't listen to what is said.

2. Moral: Luck will favour you if efforts are done.

A flood was threatening a small town, and everyone was leaving for safe ground except for one man who said, "God will save me. I have faith." As the water level rose, a jeep came to rescue him. The man refused, saying, "God will save me. I have faith." As the water level rose further, he went up to the second floor of his house, and a boat came to help him. Again he refused to go, saying, "God will save me. I have faith." The water kept rising, and the man climbed on to the roof. A helicopter came to rescue him, but he said, "God will save me. I have faith." Well, finally he drowned. When his soul reached God, he angrily questioned, "I had complete faith in you, why did you ignore my prayers and let me drown?" The Lord replied, "Who do you think sent you the jeep, the boat, and the helicopter?"

It takes action, preparation, and planning rather than wasting, wandering, and wishing to accomplish any goal in life by itself. Relying upon luck or saying you have faith in God, he will favour you and elevate you one day without any efforts is a myth.

3.   Moral: There is no easy way to get food.

Once there was a lark singing in the forest. A farmer came by with a box full of worms. The lark stopped him and asked, "What do you have in the box, and where are you going?" The farmer replied that he had worms and that he was going to the market to trade them for some feathers. The lark said, "I have many feathers. I will pluck one and give it you, and that will save me looking for worms." The farmer gave the worms to the lark, and the lark plucked a feather and gave it in return. The next day the same thing happened and day after day, on and on, until a day came that the lark had no more feathers. Now it could no longer fly to go hunting for worms. It started looking ugly and stopped singing and very soon it died out of hunger.

The moral of the story is quite clear—what the lark thought was an easy way to get food turned out to be the tougher way after all. Many times we look for an easier way, which really ends up being the tougher way after.

4. Moral: We are far behind unless we are not prepared or not doing any action.

A man bought a race horse and put him in a barn with a big sign, "The fastest horse in the world". The owner did not exercise the horse nor trained to keep it fit and in good shape. He entered the horse in a race, and it came last. The owner quickly changed the sign to "The fastest world for the horse". By inaction or not doing what should be done, people fail and they blame the luck.

5. Moral: Fear also motivates.

A company wanted to set up a pension plan. In order for the plan to be implemented, it needed 100 per cent participation. Everyone signed up except John. The plan made sense and was in the best interest of everyone. John's refusal to sign was the only obstacle. John's supervisor and other co-workers had tried, without success, to persuade him to sign. The owner of the company called John into his office and said, "John, here is a pen, and these are the papers for you to sign to enrol into the pension plan. If you don't enrol, you are fired this minute, and you will be out of the company. Right now." John took the pen, signed the papers, and while he was leaving the owner asked John why he had not signed the papers earlier. John replied, "No one explained the plan quite as clearly as you did."

    If the fear of firing and removing from the company was not there in his mind, he was reluctant to sign. But as soon as the fear motivated him, he signed without any questions because he was the only bread and butter winner for the family.

6. Moral: Choose either negative or positive from the same source.

A story of two brothers. One was a drug addict, and he was a drunk who frequently beat up his family. The other was a very successful businessman who was respected in the society and had a wonderful family. How could two brothers raised by the same parents, brought up in the same environment, be so different? The first brother was asked, "What makes you do what you do? You are a drug addict, a drunk, and you beat your family. What motivates you?" He answered, "My father. My father was a drug addict, a drunk, and beat his family. What do you expect me to be? That is what I am." The second brother was asked, "How come you are doing everything right? What is your source of motivation?" And guess what he said. "My father. When I was a little boy, I used to see my dad drunk and doing all the wrong things. I made up my mind that, that is not what I wanted to be." So the moral of the story was that both brothers derived their motivation from the same source, but one was using it positively and the other negatively.

7. Moral: A greedy person ends without enjoying anything.

A wealthy farmer was once offered all the land he could walk in a day provided he returned by sundown to the point at which he started. To get a head start, early the next morning the farmer started covering ground quickly because he wanted to get as much land as he could. Even though he was tired, he kept going all afternoon because he did not want to lose the once-in-a-lifetime opportunity to gain more wealth. Late in the afternoon, he remembered that the condition he had to fulfil to get the land was to get back to the starting point by sundown. His greed had gotten him far from the starting point. He started his returning journey, keeping an eye on how close he was to sundown. The closer it got to sundown, the faster he ran. He was exhausted and out of breath, and he pushed himself beyond the point of endurance. He collapsed upon reaching the starting point and died. He did make it before sundown. He was buried and all the land he needed was a small plot.

There is a lot of truth in the story and a lesson to be learned. Whether the farmer was wealthy or not, any greedy person would have ended the same way, at last!

8. Moral: Think considerably for self as well as others.

A ten-year-old boy went to an ice cream shop, sat at a table, and asked the waitress, "How much is an ice cream cone?" She said, "Seventy-five cents." The boy started counting the coins he had in his hand. Then he asked how much a small cup of ice cream was. The waitress impatiently replied, "Sixty-five cents." The boy said, "I will have the small ice cream cup." The boy ate his ice cream, paid the bill, and left. When the waitress came to pick up the empty plate, she was touched. Underneath the plate were ten one-cent coins left as the tip. The young boy had consideration for the waitress before he ordered his ice cream. He showed sensitivity and care. He thought of others before himself.

So always show some consideration, courtesy, and polite attitude to others so they will care for you, love you, and respect you.

9. Moral: "I feel how you feel" and "I understand how you feel" is nothing but empathy and sympathy.

A boy went to the pet store to buy a puppy. Four puppies were sitting together, priced at $50 each. Then there was one sitting alone in a corner. The boy asked if that was from the same litter, if it was for sale, and why it was sitting alone. The store owner replied that it was a deformed one and is not for sale. The boy asked what the deformity was. The store owner replied that the puppy was born without a hip socket and had a leg missing. The boy asked, "What will you do with this one?" The reply was it would be put to sleep. The boy asked if he could play with that puppy. The store owner said, "Sure." The boy picked the puppy up, and the puppy licked him on the ear. Instantly the boy decided that was the puppy he wanted to buy. The store owner said, "That's not for sale!" The boy insisted and requested; the store owner agreed. The boy pulled out $2 from his pocket and ran to get $48 from his mother. As he reached the door, the store owner shouted after him, "I don't understand why you would pay full money for this one when you could buy a good one for the same price." The boy did not say a word. He just lifted his left trouser leg, and he was wearing a brace. The pet store owner said, "I understand. Go ahead, take this one." The boy showed empathy, and the store owner showed sympathy.

10. Moral: How people remember you after your death.

About a hundred years ago, a man looked at the morning newspaper and, to his surprise and horror, read his name in the obituary column. The newspaper had reported his death by mistake. His first response was shock. Am I here or there? When he regained his composure, his next thought was to find out what people had said about him. The obituary read, "Dynamite King Dies", and "He was the merchant of death". This man was the inventor of dynamite, and when he read the words "Merchant of death", he asked himself, "Is this how I am going to be remembered?" He decided that this was not the way he wanted to be remembered. From that day on, he started working towards peace. He, the Dynamite King, was Alfred Nobel, and he is remembered today by the great Nobel prizes. Just as Alfred Nobel redefined his values, you should step back and do the same.

11. Moral: Is your life worth living?

A boy was drowning in a river, and he shouted for help. A man passing by jumped in the river and saved the boy's life. As the man was leaving, the boy said, "Thank you." The man asked, "For what?" The boy replied, "For saving my life." The man looked into the boy's eyes and said, "Son, make sure when you grow up that your life was worth saving."

This is a wake-up call. It is time to think. Success without fulfilment is meaningless unless there is a sense of meaning and purpose. Life is empty and unhappy regardless of how much prestige, money, or education you have.

12. Moral: The responsibility of parenting.

A judge, when sentencing a man for robbery, asked if he had anything to say. The man replied, "Yes, Your Honour, please sentence my parents to jail also." The judge asked, "Why?" The prisoner answered, "When I was a little boy, I stole a pencil from school. My parents knew about it but never said a word. Then I stole a pen, they knowingly ignored it. I continued to steal many other things from the school and the neighbourhood till it became an obsession. They knew about it, yet they never said a word. If anyone belongs in jail with me, they do."

He is right, although it does not absolve him of his responsibility, the question is, did the parents do their job right? Obviously not. Giving choices to children is important, but choices without directions result in disaster. Complete mental and physical preparation is the result of sacrifice and self-discipline.

"A tree can make one lakh match sticks, but one match stick can burn one lakh trees." In the same way, a single wrongdoing will one day become your habit and then character. So always nurture the habit of educating your children of what is wrong in life and what is right! Be in a higher conscious state of mind!

13. Moral: Internal motivation is the inner gratification, not for success or winning but for the fulfilment that comes from having done it.

Coach to a player: "Son, how could I have been so wrong? I have never seen you play like this before. What happened? How did you play so well? I have no confidence in you, so I have kept you as the last player? How could you do this?"

The boy replied, "Coach, my father is watching me today." The coach turned around and looked at the place where the boy's father used to sit. There was no one there. He said, "Son, your father used to sit there when you came for practice, but I don't see anyone there today." The boy replied, "Coach, there is something I never told you. My father was blind. Just four days ago, he died. Today is the first day he is watching me from above." Internal motivation is the inner gratification, not for success or winning but for the fulfilment that comes from having done it.

14. Moral: Never put a mask, be what you are.

A young executive with poor self-esteem was promoted, but he could not reconcile himself to his new office and position. There was a knock at his door. To show how important and busy he was, he picked up the phone and then asked the visitor to come in. As the man waited for the executive, the executive kept talking on the phone, nodding and saying, "No problem, I can handle that." After a few minutes, he hung up and asked the visitor what he could do for him. The man replied, "Sir, I am here to connect your phone."

15. Moral: You are what God made you to be, so don't get complex, love yourself and serve the mankind.

There was a potter who had two pots for him for getting the water for food and drink. Out of both the pots, one had a little crack in it. The potter used to take the pots daily tied to the stick, with two pots on both ends. The pot which was without any crack used to abuse the cracked pot, saying that "You are fit for nothing, nor can you give our master the full water for his hardship, and your water gets leaked throughout in the path." By listening daily, the cracked pot one day thought, *Whatever my brother pot is saying is a fact, and I must end myself so that the master shall make a new and good pot like the other pot.* The next morning when the master went to pick up the pots for water, the cracked pot told the master, "I have no worthiness or usefulness to you, so you better break me and make a new pot for yourself which will give you the full water." The master understood the feeling of the cracked pot and said, "Let me show you something first, and if you feel you are correct, I will break you." The master took both the pots to the pond and filled the pots with water. On his return journey to the house, he walked half the way and stopped and said, "Now listen, I agree that the strong pot gave me a pot full of water, but my other cracked pot did not give me a pot full of water, but he gave lush green grass throughout the path. A period ago there were thorny bushes here and pointed stones which used to pierce my legs, and I used to bleed profusely daily, but now, see my legs. I have no injuries any more because by daily leaking water throughout the path, the lush green grass has become my velvet passage, and without any pain, I can do the job and at the same time, the pot is watering the grass to keep them green growing. Now if you feel you are not fit for anything, after going home I will break you." The cracked pot said, "I am sorry. I was unable to know the comforts God gave you because of my weakness. Therefore forgive me and please do not break me. I will be happy to serve you as I am."

16. Moral: Comparing and postponing the happiness will not allow you to enjoy the present.

A mother had two daughters, and the elder was studying in tenth grade and the younger was in eight. The younger daughter had a habit of comparing herself with her elder sister. One day when the elder sister passed her tenth exam and started her college, seeing the younger sister was not happy, the mother asked, "Why are you not happy that your elder sister has passed tenth and joined college?" She replied, "I will be happy only when I pass my tenth exam and when I will join college because I love very colourful dresses and not this school uniform." Mother said, "My dear daughter, for that you need to wait for two years because you are in eight." She replied, "No problem, I am ready to wait till I pass my tenth and join the college." After two years, her elder sister joined the degree college, and the younger passed the tenth and joined the college, but after joining the college, she was not happy because she wanted to join degree like her elder sister. Therefore, she was not happy in her intermediate college. After three years, her elder sister had completed the degree, and the mother saw an alliance for her and marriage was fixed and the marriage day. Her younger sister was asked by Mother, "Are you not happy that your sister is getting married?" She replied, "No, I will be happy, when I complete my degree and I will be married." Two years passed, the younger daughter also finished her degree and had an alliance and she was married. The elder daughter had given birth to a boy child, and the mother and younger daughter visited the hospital. After seeing the baby, Mother was very happy and asked her younger daughter, "Are you not happy that your sister has given birth to such a beautiful boy?" Then she replied, "No. I will be happy when I will give birth to a beautiful boy like sister has given." After a year, she gave birth to a child more beautiful than her sister's son. Many years passed and her mother also passed away, and one day when she stood before the mirror, she noticed that her hair has turned white. The children have grown up, and in comparison and by postponing the happiness, she has come to an old age. Now, she was able to realise that by comparing herself to her sister, she was postponing the happiness of her life from age thirteen to forties. Thereafter she stopped comparing herself with the sister and enjoyed each and every day of life with her husband and grown-up children, and thereafter they lived happily ever after.

17. Moral: Never be proud of anything or else you will be under the feet.

In a riverbank, there was a rock and a few metres away, on one of the plant, there was a very beautiful flower. The flower used to laugh at the rock, saying, "How ugly you are and how incapable you are. The waves are hitting on you, and you are unable to do anything. I really feel very pity for you." After some days, the river dried up, and the rocks were very black and soft that a sculptor took it home and made statues of gods and sold the same to the temples. The statues were installed, and people came with flowers to give to the deity, and the priest used to put them at the feet of the deity. The rock (deity) even now never told anything to the flower, and the flower understood that it was proud of its beauty and laughing at someone else's situation has brought him to the feet of the rock.